CHRIS CALDICOTT is a food and travel writer who has travelled to
over a hundred countries in search of recipes and food stories.
With his wife Carolyn he founded the World Food Café in London's Covent Garden
and they have written many books together including *World Food Café*,
World Food Café: Quick and Easy, *The Spice Routes* and *Vintage Tea Party*,
all published by Frances Lincoln. This is his first book for children.

For Maya – C.C.

First published in Great Britain in 2012 and in the USA in 2013 by Frances
Lincoln Children's Books, 74-77 White Lion Street,
London, N1 9PF
www.franceslincoln.com

This paperback edition first published in Great Britain and in the USA in 2015

A CIP catalogue record for this book is available from the British Library.

ISBN 978-1-84780-653-6

Set in Scala Sans

Printed in China

9 8 7 6 5 4 3 2 1

World Food
Alphabet

Chris **C**aldico**t**t

Frances Lincoln
Children's Books

AUTHOR'S NOTE

Food is an important part of life for every person, every day, all over the world. The sort of food people eat, and the way they eat it, buy it, cook it and prepare it varies greatly around the world.

Something we all share, though, is the need for a good diet to keep us strong and healthy. For some this is more of a challenge than for others. *World Food Alphabet* is a global A to Z of different foods, and ways of eating, gathering and preparing them. From Asia to Europe and from Africa to the Americas, it looks at the ways children and their families cook and consume food, and a variety of the ingredients we all use one way or another.

Chris Caldicott

A a *is for* APRICOTS

Apricots are a small, sweet and juicy orange fruit that grow on trees in countries with a warm climate, where they are eaten fresh. Most apricots, like these in the Hunza Valley in Pakistan, are dried in the sun before having their stones removed so they can be transported and stored more easily. Dried apricots can be eaten as a delicious and nutritious alternative to sweets.

B b *is for* BANANAS

Bananas grow on trees in tropical countries, where they are picked and sold in bunches. Marlon on the island of St Vincent in the Caribbean is helping his father sell bananas from a stall on the beach to passers-by fancying a healthy snack. In countries where bananas grow, people sometimes use their leaves to wrap food in and carry it home from the market. They can also be used instead of plates to eat food from, which means no washing up!

C c *is for*
COCONUTS

Coconuts are actually a fruit with a hard stone, and not a nut at all. Fresh, young coconuts are full of liquid that makes a sweet and refreshing drink and their flesh is creamy. As they get older, the flesh hardens to become white and nutty. Coconuts grow high up in palm trees, like these ones in Sri Lanka, that have to be climbed so the fruit can be cut from the branches. Hard coconut flesh can be grated and used to flavour cakes and biscuits, or soaked in water and strained to make coconut milk for cooking.

D d is for
DATES

Dates, like these on sale in a market in Morocco, are a very important food for people who live in hot, dry countries. The trees they come from are found in deserts, where almost nothing else can grow. They are a very sweet fruit which people eat as a nutritious snack or use in cooking as a healthy alternative to sugar. Dates can be eaten either fresh or dried. Dried dates remain edible for many years so are very useful for people who move around a lot.

E e is for
EGGS

People eat eggs all over the world. Eggs like these ones on sale in a farmer's market in France can be eaten boiled, fried, poached or scrambled, or mixed with other things and made into an omelette. They are also used to make cakes and puddings. As a food, they are an important source of protein, especially for people who don't eat much meat.

F f *is for* FISH

Fish are the world's largest source of wild food.
For people like Angelo, who lives on an island off the coast of Mozambique in southern Africa, fish are a daily food. His family sell any spare fish they catch to people who don't have time to catch their own. Even though the world's seas, rivers and lakes are full of fish, we have to be careful not to take too many out. We must make sure there are always enough left for people who can't easily get other types of food.

G g *is for* GOATS

Goats are an important source of food for many people, not just as meat, but also for their milk, which can be drunk or used to make butter, cheese and yoghurt. The children of this Samburu family in Kenya spend the days when they are not at school looking after their family's goats while they graze in the bush. They keep them safe from wild animals and make sure none of them get lost.

H h *is for* HONEY

Honey was used to sweeten food long before we started using sugar, and still makes a much healthier alternative. It is made from the nectar of flowers, gathered by bees and stored in honeycombs. In some countries people gather honey from the nests of wild bees high up in trees, but in others it comes from hives built so it can be more easily harvested, then sold in jars, like these on sale in a market in Mexico.

I i *is for* ICE

In many parts of the world where not everyone has a fridge, ice is the main way of keeping food fresh. Without ice, lots of food would be spoilt before people had the chance to eat it. Fishermen, like this one in Bangladesh, buy ice in big blocks to keep their catch fresh while it is transported to market. In other countries people store their food in fridges for the same reason, to keep it cool so it lasts longer.

J j is for JOURNEYS

Every meal requires a journey. Ingredients often travel huge distances from where they are grown to where they are sold. People then have to travel from where they live to buy them. For some this might be a drive to the supermarket, a walk to a local street market, or a boat ride to the nearest town. Some people, like Sarita (left), who lives in a mountain village in Nepal, this lady in the Thar Desert in India (centre) and this Kenyan woman (right) have to walk every day to a well just to collect water, the most essential ingredient of any meal.

Kk is for KITCHENS

Food is prepared and cooked in kitchens. Some kitchens, like this one in London (bottom right) have hot and cold running water from taps, and electricity to power cookers, fridges and other gadgets. Others, like these three in a small village in the Rajasthan desert, are much more basic. Here food is cooked over an open fire, and water and other ingredients are collected daily and stored in pots. The most useful gadget is a stone grinder. The kitchen is usually the most important room in any home, as it is where food is prepared and where families gather to share meals.

Ll is for LEMONS & LIMES

Lemons and limes are citrus fruits, rich in vitamin C. Their juice can be used to make drinks such as lemonade, salad dressings, and as a marinade to make fish and meat more tender and tasty. Rahul's family sells limes from this market stall in Malaysia, where people squeeze them over fruit salads and also use lime leaves to add flavour to cooked dishes. In North Africa, people chop them up and dip them in hot water to soften the peel, then cook them in stews.

Mm *is for* MARKETS

Street markets, like these in Morocco (bottom right), Guatemala (bottom middle) and Burma (bottom left), are where most people around the world buy food. They are often noisy and colourful places, where customers choose what they want, then bargain to get the best price. Others go to farmers' markets, like these in France (top right) and England (top middle). Buying food in supermarkets, like this one in London (top left), where everything has a fixed price saves time, but is much less fun!

Nn is for NOODLES

Noodles, usually made from rice or wheat flour, are a popular food all over Asia, where, like on this street stall in Thailand (bottom left) and the cafe in Vietnam (bottom right), they are often mixed with other ingredients to make a filling soup. They can also be fried with meat, fish, or vegetables, or just boiled and eaten on their own with a sauce. Pasta is a European version of noodles, also made from flour dough in many different shapes and sizes and eaten with a sauce.

O o *is for* OLIVES

Olives are the fruit of a tree that grows all around the Mediterranean Sea, where people have been eating them almost every day for thousands of years. Olives, like these being sold by Ali in Morocco, can be either black or green. They can be eaten raw in salads, cooked in stews or grilled on pizzas. Olives are also crushed to make olive oil, which can be used as a salad dressing or to fry food.

Pp *is for* PINEAPPLES

Pineapples are one of the world's biggest fruits. These three girls in Bali are taking pineapples to the market in bowls balanced on their heads. As pineapples are so heavy and spiky, this is the most comfortable way of carrying them, after a bit of practice. Lots of pineapples end up in tins so that they can be transported and preserved, but they are much better eaten fresh. Eating fresh fruit is an important part of any healthy diet.

Qq is for QUANTITIES

Whenever people buy food they have to decide on the quantity they need. In places where food is sold in markets, like this one in Hanoi, Vietnam, shoppers choose the produce they want, before it is weighed on scales to work out the price. In supermarkets, most food is sold in packets that have already been weighed and priced. It is important not to buy too much fresh food in case it spoils before it is eaten and gets wasted.

Rr *is for*
RICE

Rice is a daily food for almost half the people in the world and an essential ingredient of every meal for them. It grows very easily in hot countries with plenty of rainfall, in fields such as this one in southern China. As a food it provides lots of energy but has little taste, so it is often eaten with spicy dishes of vegetables, meat or fish, and used to soak up the sauce. It can also be cooked with milk and sugar as a pudding, or ground to make flour.

Ss _is for_
SPICES

Spices are used in cooking to make food tastier. Most are seeds and powders, like these on sale in a market in Tunisia; others are made from barks, roots and fruits. In many countries people add spices to almost every dish, in others they only use them occasionally. Some spices, like chillies, can make dishes taste hot, but most just add flavour and nutrition.

Tt _is for_ TOMATOES

Tomatoes can be eaten raw, made into a sauce, chutney or juice, or used in cooking. They are a popular food all around the world, as they can be grown in almost any climate. In colder countries they have to be grown in greenhouses. This man in Durban, South Africa, has so many to sell that he has time to read a book between customers.

U u *is for* UTENSILS

Utensils such as pots and pans, or knives and forks, are used to cook and eat food. Without utensils, cooking would be impossible. Ingredients need to be chopped with knives, then fried, baked or boiled in pans, woks, trays or pots, before being served with spoons and eaten from plates. In many places people just use their hands to eat food, in some they use chopsticks, and in others knives and forks. This lady in Mali (left) is selling ladles for serving and stirring, and the man in Pakistan (right) iron griddles for cooking on.

V v *is for*

VEGETABLES

Eating lots of vegetables, like these on display in a market in Spain, is one of the best ways to stay healthy. Fresh vegetables should be a part of everybody's diet every day. They can be eaten as part of a meal with meat or fish, or with rice, noodles or beans, or made into soups and salads, or just eaten on their own. Many people around the world who never eat meat still manage to live perfectly healthy lives on a vegetarian diet.

W w *is for* WATER

Without water there would be no food. Every plant, fish, animal and person needs water to live. We have to be very careful with the world's water and make sure everybody has enough to drink, wash, water their crops and give to their animals. Not everyone has the luxury of getting clean water from a tap, many people, such as Anita, who lives in a village in Bengal, have to collect it every day from a village pump or a river, then carry it home and boil it to make it safe to drink.

X x is for OXEN

Oxen, like these ones in a field in Burma, are working animals. Even today, most farmers around the world can't afford modern tractors, so they use animals such as oxen to plough the fields where they grow food, and to transport the crops they harvest. Oxen are so strong that they are also used to power mills where there is no electricity. They walk around in a circle to turn the heavy stones used to crush grains such as wheat.

Y y is for YAMS

Yams are a popular food in South America, Asia, Africa and the Caribbean. They are a root crop or tuber, like potatoes. This family in the Caribbean are peeling yams before they cook them. Like potatoes, they cannot be eaten raw, so have to be boiled, fried or baked, or turned into flour which people sprinkle over their food.

Zz *is for* ZUCCHINI

Zucchini is the Italian and American name for the vegetable known elsewhere as a courgette. Zucchini can be poached, stuffed, baked, fried or cut into narrow strips and eaten raw in salads. The yellow flowers of a zucchini, like these on sale in Venice, can be stuffed and deep-fried as a delicacy.

MORE BOOKS BY CHRIS CALDICOTT FROM FRANCES LINCOLN

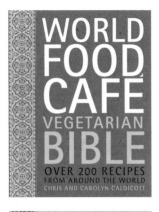

WORLD FOOD CAFÉ: VEGETARIAN BIBLE
Over 200 Recipes from Around the World
by Carolyn Caldicott and Chris Caldicott

Chris and Carolyn Caldicott are the godparents of global vegetarian cuisine in the UK. For twenty years their World Food Cafe in London's Covent Garden was the hub of new flavours, colours and combinations in vegetarian cooking. *World Food Café: Vegetarian Bible* collects the best recipes from two decades of globetrotting, tried and tested to be easy to make at home.
'Tasty recipes that are an antidote to the blandness of many vegetarian meals.' *Independent*

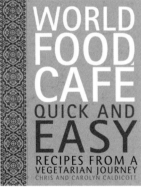

WORLD FOOD CAFÉ: QUICK AND EASY
Recipes from a Vegetarian Journey
by Carolyn Caldicott and Chris Caldicott

This book brings together the recipes Chris and Carolyn Caldicott collected on a trek across the Andes; on their way down the Ganges delta; in the mountain kingdom of Bhutan; in the remote jungle of upper Burma; and even further away. All the recipes are quick and easy to cook, ideal for life on the road or for a simple, quick and healthy meal after a busy day. With over 100 entirely vegetarian recipes from across the globe and stunning travel and food photography throughout, *World Food Café: Quick and Easy* is the ultimate cookbook for preparing delicious world vegetarian food at home.

BOMBAY LUNCHBOX
by Carolyn Caldicott and Chris Caldicott

Renowned for her imaginative yet accessible recipes, Carolyn Caldicott combines anecdotes and recipes from Anglo-Indian cookery with the culture of the 'Tiffin' lunchbox, cooked at home and delivered to the workplace in characteristic stainless steel tiered tins. Carolyn's collection of sweet and savoury vegetarian recipes for lunch, afternoon tea or any snack eaten between breakfast and dinner, will appeal to anyone who loves India and Indian food.

Frances Lincoln titles are available from all good bookshops.
You can also buy books and find out more about your favourite titles,
authors and illustrators on our website: www.franceslincoln.com